Pre-Algebra

Table of Contents

Cover art: ©Glowimages, Getty Images

ISBN 978-1-4168-6038-9
218448

ADVENTURE!

Cooking in the Mountains

©Martial Colomb, Getty Images

Some people in the United States live in the mountains high above sea level. Sea level is the level of the oceans. It takes longer to cook food at heights above sea level because the air contains less oxygen. A recipe that works closer to sea level may not work at a higher altitude, or height.

Boiling Point

In this adventure, you will find the boiling point of water at different altitudes above sea level. Answer each problem.

1 Sea level is at 0 feet. At 0 feet, the boiling point of water is 212°F. For each increase in height by 500 feet, the boiling point of water lowers by about 1°F. Complete the second column of the input-output table to show the boiling point of water at different altitudes by subtracting 1 from the previous boiling point.

Altitude, x (ft)	Boiling Point, y (°F)	(x, y)
0	212	(0, 212)
500		
1,000		
1,500		
2,000		
2,500		
3,000		
3,500		

2 Complete the last column of the input-output table by creating the ordered pair for each.

3 Graph each point from the input-output table in the coordinate plane on the next page. Use a straightedge to draw a line through the points.

4 Is the slope of the line positive, negative, or 0? Use the graph in problem 3 to find the slope of the line.

Further Adventure

5 Extend the graph in problem 3 to find the altitude when water boils at 202°F.

Cooking at High Altitudes

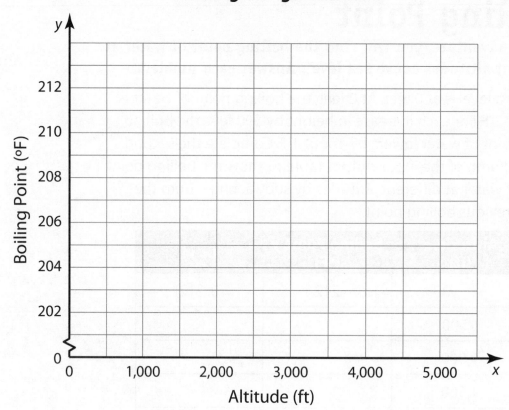

New Vocabulary
base
exponent

Exponents

Name _____ Class _____ Date _____

GET STARTED

1   **a.** $3 \times 3 =$ _____   **b.** $^-4 \times {}^-4 =$ _____   **c.** $^-5 \times {}^-5 \times {}^-5 =$ _____

       base   exponent

2   **a.** $4 \times 4 = \boxed{}^{\boxed{}}$ **b.** $^-5 \times {}^-5 \times {}^-5 = (\boxed{})^{\boxed{}}$

3 $2^3 = \boxed{} \times \boxed{} \times \boxed{}$

       $= \boxed{}$

4 $(^-2)^3 = \boxed{} \times \boxed{} \times \boxed{}$

       $= \boxed{}$

5 $^-(2)^3 = {}^-1 \times \boxed{} \times \boxed{} \times \boxed{}$

       $= {}^-1 \times \boxed{}$

       $= \boxed{}$

6 $3^4 = \boxed{} \times \boxed{} \times \boxed{} \times \boxed{}$

       $= \boxed{}$

BUILD THE CONCEPT

Suppose Mark, Claire, Maria, and Tom each call 4 different friends. The friends who are called then each call 4 different friends. How many phone calls are made in this last round? Assume no friend received more than one call.

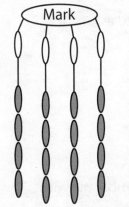 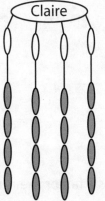 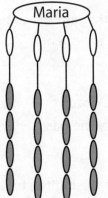 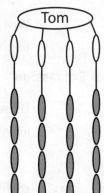

Mark   Claire   Maria   Tom

$4 \times 4 =$ _____

$=$ _____

_____ $\times 4 \times 4 =$ _____

$=$ _____

The model shows _____ groups of 4×4.

There are _____ phone calls made in the last round.

TRY IT TOGETHER

Write each product as an exponential expression.

7 $6 \times 6 \times 6 \times 6 =$ ☐☐

8 $^-1 \times {}^-1 \times {}^-1 \times {}^-1 \times {}^-1 =$ (☐)☐

Find the value of each exponential expression.

9 $(^-5)^2 =$ ☐ $\times$ ☐

$=$ ☐

10 $^-(3)^3 = {}^-1 \times$ ☐ $\times$ ☐ $\times$ ☐

$= {}^-1 \times$ ☐

$=$ ☐

WORK ON YOUR OWN

HOW TO

Write an Exponential Expression

Using Symbols	Using Words
1. $7 \times 7 \times 7$ base $= 7$	Write the repeated factor as the base.
2. exponent $= 3$ $7 \times 7 \times 7 = 7^3$	Write the number of times the base is used as a factor as the exponent.

Evaluate an Exponential Expression

Using Symbols	Using Words
1. 3^5 base $= 3$	Identify the base.
2. $3 \times 3 \times 3 \times 3 \times 3 = 243$	Multiply using the base as a factor the number of times indicated by the exponent.

Go to
VmathLive.com

<u>Module</u> Pre-Algebra
<u>Activity</u> Exponents

Vmath_{LIVE}

Lesson 1

SKILL BUILDING:
NEW AND REVIEW

Write each product as an exponential expression.

11 $10 \times 10 \times 10$

12 $^-11 \times ^-11 \times ^-11$

13 $^-6 \times ^-6 \times ^-6 \times ^-6$

14 3×3

15 $^-1 \times 4 \times 4 \times 4$

16 $7 \times 7 \times 7 \times 7 \times 7$

Find the value of each exponential expression.

17 9^2

18 4^3

19 $^-(5)^2$

20 $(^-8)^2$

21 $^-(7)^2$

22 $(^-9)^3$

PROBLEM-SOLVING:
NEW AND REVIEW

Solve each problem.

23 Is $(^-4)^2$ the same as $^-(4)^2$? Explain.

24 The formula to find the volume of a cube that has dimensions of 3 inches on each side is $3 \times 3 \times 3$. How is this expression written using an exponent?

25 Joe has 64 baseball cards. He says that he has 2^6 baseball cards. Is he correct?

26 Maria tosses 3 number cubes with sides labeled 1–6. There are 6^3 possible number combinations that she could roll. What is the value of 6^3?

CHECK UP

Answer each question.

1 Which expression represents
$^-5 \times {}^-5 \times {}^-5 \times {}^-5$?

    a. $(^-5)^3$ **b.** $(^-5)^4$

    c. 4^6 **d.** $^-(5)^3$

2 What is the value of $(^-2)^5$?

    a. $^-8$ **b.** 25

    c. $^-32$ **d.** 32

3 Which two answer choices in problem 2 are the least reasonable? Explain.

_____

_____

_____

There are more than 10^{11} stars in the Milky Way galaxy. Is this more or less than
$10 \times 10 \times 10 \times 10 \times 10 \times 10$? Explain.

_____

_____

_____

4 Which of these values has a base of 7?
$(7)^2$ or $^-(2)^7$

_____

_____

Variables and Expressions

Name _____ Class _____ Date _____

GET STARTED

1 ⁻3 + 4 = _____

2 ⁻3 + n, when $n = 4$

⁻3 + n = ⁻3 + _____

= _____

3 3 × k _____ _____

4 6m, when $m = 11$

6m = _____ × _____

= _____

5 $\frac{t}{9}$, when $t = 4.5$

$\frac{t}{9} = \frac{}{9}$

= _____

6 39 + u, when $u = $ ⁻41

39 + u = _____ + _____

= _____

7 $c - 17$, when $c = 24$

$c - 17$ = _____ − _____

= _____

BUILD THE CONCEPT

Phrase	Algebraic Expression	Value when $n = 24$
3 more than a number	$n + 3$	
5 less than a number	$n - 5$	
8 times a number	$8n$	
A number divided by 6	$n \div 6$	

TRY IT TOGETHER

Evaluate each expression.

8 $^-8 \cdot x$, when $x = ^-12$

$^-8 \cdot x =$ _____ $\times$ _____

$=$ _____

9 $\dfrac{j}{16}$, when $j = 48$

$\dfrac{j}{16} = \dfrac{\boxed{}}{16}$

$=$ _____

10 $t + 45$, when $t = 82$

$t + 45 =$ _____ $+$ _____

$=$ _____

11 $k - 61$, when $k = 73$

$k - 61 =$ _____ $-$ _____

$=$ _____

WORK ON YOUR OWN

Evaluate an Expression with a Variable

HOW TO

Using Symbols	Using Words
1. $6n$, when $n = ^-9$ $6n = 6 \times ^-9$	Substitute the given value for the variable in the expression.
2. $6 \times ^-9 = ^-54$	Evaluate the expression.

SKILL BUILDING: NEW AND REVIEW

Evaluate each expression.

12 $34z$, when $z = 6$

13 $\dfrac{b}{13}$, when $b = {}^-78$

14 $g + 54$, when $g = 74$

15 $8 \cdot m$, when $m = {}^-20$

16 $7.8a$, when $a = 0.3$

17 $4h$, when $h = 2$

18 $y - 94$, when $y = 21$

19 $\dfrac{j}{2}$, when $j = {}^-36$

20 $\dfrac{c}{4}$, when $c = {}^-24$

Find the value of each exponential expression.

21 ${}^-(3)^3$

22 1^6

23 $({}^-6)^4$

PROBLEM-SOLVING

Using a 4-Step Plan

Mark and Nate played a game. Nate's score was 3 times as much as Mark's score. If Mark scored m points, write an expression to show how many points Nate scored.

a. **Find:** an expression to show Nate's score

b. **How?** Use the 4-Step Plan to find the relationship between Mark's and Nate's scores.

c. **Solve.**

Nate: 3 times Mark's score

Mark: _____ points

Nate's score: 3 times as much as Mark's

_____   ☐   _____

If Mark's score is m, Nate's score is _____ or _____ or _____.

d. **Is the answer reasonable? Explain.** _____

_____

PROBLEM-SOLVING: NEW AND REVIEW

Solve each problem.

24 Eva and Jen are sisters. Eva is 7 years older than Jen. If Jen's age is *n*, how old is Eva?

25 William carved 2 times as many wooden ducks as Fran. If *r* represents the number of wooden ducks Fran carved, what expression represents the number of wooden ducks William carved?

26 Is $(^-3)^3$ the same as $^-(3)^3$? Explain.

27 The temperature yesterday was 11°F cooler than it was today. If *t* represents the temperature today, what expression represents the temperature yesterday? What was the temperature yesterday if today's temperature is 68°F ?

CHECK UP

Answer each question.

1 What is $\dfrac{y}{3.5}$ when $y = 7$?

   a. 0.2   **b.** 0.5

   c. 2   **d.** 24.5

2 What is $^-78 - u$ when $u = {}^-55$?

   a. 23   **b.** $^-23$

   c. 133   **d.** $^-133$

3 Explain how to find the answer to problem 2. _____

_____

_____

_____

_____

4 If Andrew's dad is 4 times as old as Andrew, write an expression to show his age. Solve the expression if Andrew is 8 years old.

_____

_____

_____

Evaluating Expressions Using Order of Operations

Name _____ Class _____ Date _____

GET STARTED

1 $5 - \dfrac{14}{7} =$ _____ $-$ _____ $=$ _____

2 $5 - \dfrac{r}{7}$, when $r = 14$

$5 - \dfrac{r}{7} =$ _____ $- \dfrac{}{} =$ _____

3 $^-6(d + 2)^2$, when $d = 3$

$^-6(d + 2)^2 = ^-6 \times ($ _____ $+ 2)^2$

$= ^-6 \times$ _____ ^{2}

$= ^-6 \times$ _____

$=$ _____

4 $\dfrac{n + 5}{10 - 7}$, when $n = 3.7$

$\dfrac{n + 5}{10 - 7} = \dfrac{ + 5}{10 - 7}$

$= \dfrac{}{}$

$=$ _____

5 $(5 + 9) - t^3$, when $t = 2$

$(5 + 9) - t^3 = (5 + 9) -$ ▢ ^{3}

$=$ _____ $-$ _____ ^{3}

$=$ _____ $-$ _____

$=$ _____

6 $2m + 5^2$, when $m = ^-12$

$2m + 5^2 = 2 \times$ _____ $+ 5^2$

$= 2 \times$ _____ $+$ _____

$=$ _____ $+$ _____

$=$ _____

BUILD THE CONCEPT

Henry is asked to write a numerical expression with a value of 32. He starts to write an expression but cannot decide where to place parentheses. Help Henry place parentheses in the expression. The parentheses should enclose two numbers and one operation.

$$12 + 9 \times 3 - 7$$

Try $(12 + 9) \times 3 - 7$.

_____ $\times 3 - 7$

_____ $- 7 =$ _____

Try $12 + (9 \times 3) - 7$.

$12 +$ _____ $- 7$

_____ $- 7 =$ _____

Parentheses should be placed around _____.

TRY IT TOGETHER

Evaluate each expression.

7 $(10 - 4.6) + s^2$, when $s = 4$

$(10 - 4.6) + s^2 = (10 - 4.6) + \underline{\hspace{1cm}}^2$

$= \underline{\hspace{1cm}} + \underline{\hspace{1cm}}^2$

$= \underline{\hspace{1cm}} + \underline{\hspace{1cm}}$

$= \underline{\hspace{1cm}}$

8 $\dfrac{^-3(^-9 + 3)}{p}$, when $p = ^-2$

$\dfrac{^-3(^-9 + 3)}{p} = \dfrac{^-3 \times (^-9 + 3)}{}$

$= \dfrac{^-3 \times }{}$

$= \dfrac{}{}$.

$= \underline{\hspace{1cm}}$

WORK ON YOUR OWN

HOW TO

Evaluate an Expression Using Order of Operations

Using Symbols	Using Words
1. $7 + 3 \times t^2$, when $t = 5$ $7 + 3 \times t^2 = 7 + 3 \times \mathbf{5}^2$	Substitute the value of the variable into the expression.
2. $ = 7 + 3 \times \mathbf{25}$ $ = 7 + \mathbf{75}$ $ = \mathbf{82}$	Follow the order of operations to evaluate the numerical expression. Perform operations inside parentheses. Evaluate exponential expressions. Multiply and divide from left to right. Add and subtract from left to right.
$\dfrac{3 \times 4 + 12}{20 - 2^3} = \dfrac{24}{12} = 2$	When a problem has a fractional expression, first evaluate above and below the fraction bar separately. Then divide the numerator by the denominator.

Go to
VmathLive.com

Module Pre-Algebra
Activities Order of Operations 2
Simple Substitution 2

Vmath LIVE

Lesson 3

SKILL BUILDING: NEW AND REVIEW

Evaluate each expression.

9 $16 - (^-3 + b)^2$, when $b = ^-1$

10 $\dfrac{3(7 + a)}{^-2}$, when $a = ^-3$

11 $\dfrac{^-20}{w} + (^-3)^2$, when $w = ^-4$

12 $3(9 - s^2)$, when $s = 2$

13 $2(k + 2)$, when $k = 7.8$

14 $\dfrac{4(1 + t)}{^-10}$, when $t = 4$

15 $\dfrac{8 + 4(7)}{s + ^-4}$, when $s = ^-5$

16 $4 + x - \dfrac{3(2^2)}{2}$, when $x = 3$

17 $7 + 3b$, when $b = ^-12$

Find each sum, product, or quotient.

18 $^-7 \times 8$

19 $\dfrac{^-54}{6}$

20 $9 + ^-12$

PROBLEM-SOLVING: NEW AND REVIEW

Solve each problem.

21 The expression $\dfrac{(f - 32)}{1.8}$ can be used to convert a temperature in degrees Fahrenheit to a temperature in degrees Celsius. The variable f represents the temperature in degrees Fahrenheit. What is the temperature in degrees Celsius when the temperature is 50°F?

22 Ben and his sister collect quarters. They have saved $15 in quarters. How many quarters do they have?

23 The expression $s^2 - 8^2$ can be used to find the area of Sheila's countertop in her square kitchen. The variable s represents the length of Sheila's kitchen. What is the area of Sheila's countertop in square feet if the length of her kitchen is 10 feet?

24 Kim will spend $20 + 3s$ dollars on a pair of jeans and 3 shirts that cost s dollars each. How much will her total bill be if each shirt costs $25? If Kim has $90 will she have enough money? Explain.

CHECK UP

Answer each question.

1 What is $16 - 3.2m$ when $m = 2$?

    a. 25.6   **b.** ⁻48

    c. 10   **d.** 9.6

2 What is $\dfrac{^-4}{^-1 + z}$ when $z = 5$?

    a. 0   **b.** 1

    c. ⁻1   **d.** $3\dfrac{4}{5}$

3 For problem 2, what operation is performed first? Explain.

_____

_____

_____

_____

Explain how to find the value of $(5 + 7) - \dfrac{3(x)^3}{6}$ when $x = 2$.

_____

_____

_____

_____

_____

4 Write an algebraic expression that includes the variable b, exponents, and at least two different operations. Include the value of the variable b. Then evaluate the expression for the given value of b.

_____

_____

Solving Equations Using Algebra Tiles

Name _____ Class _____ Date _____

GET READY

1

_____

2

_____

3 $3 + {}^-3 =$ _____

4 ${}^-2 + 2 =$ _____

DISCOVER

5 $x + 4 = 6$

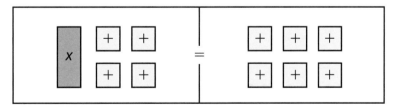

number of yellow tiles on left
side = _____

number of yellow tiles on right
side = _____

Remove _____ yellow tiles from each side.

number of yellow tiles remaining on
left side = _____

number of yellow tiles remaining on
right side = _____

$x =$ _____

6 $x - 2 = 7$

number of red tiles on left side = _____

number of yellow tiles on right side = _____

Add _____ yellow tiles and _____ red tiles to the right side.

Remove _____ red tiles from each side.

number of red tiles on remaining on left side = _____

number of yellow tiles on remaining on right side = _____

$x =$ _____

DISCOVER BOX

Why is it important to perform an operation on both sides of an equation?

_____

Why do you sometimes have to add zero pairs before you can remove the same number from each side?

_____

_____

EXPLORE MORE

Use algebra tiles to model and solve each equation for x.

7 $x + 5 = 9$ $x =$ _____

8 $x - 1 = 6$ $x =$ _____

Solving One-Step Equations Using Addition and Subtraction

Name _____ Class _____ Date _____

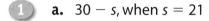

1 **a.** $30 - s$, when $s = 21$

$30 - s = 30 -$ _____

$=$ _____

b. $b + 10$, when $b = {}^-8$

$b + 10 =$ _____ $+ 10$

$=$ _____

c. $3 + n$, when $n = {}^-12$

$3 + n = 3 +$ _____

$=$ _____

2 $s + 7 = \quad 12$

$\underline{}$
$-\quad -$

$s =$

Check: $s + 7 = 12$

_____ $+ 7 \overset{?}{=} 12$

_____ $\overset{\checkmark}{=} 12$

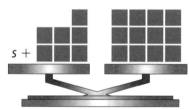

$s + 7 = 12$

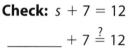

$s = 5$

3 ${}^-6 \;= r - 4$

$\underline{++}$

$= r$

Check: ${}^-6 = r - 4$

${}^-6 \overset{?}{=}$ _____ $- 4$

${}^-6 \overset{?}{=}$ _____ $+$ _____

${}^-6 =$ _____

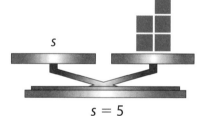

BUILD THE CONCEPT

Look at the equation modeled by the algebra tiles.

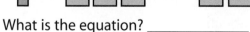

What is the equation? _____

How many ones tiles must be removed from each side? _____

What remains on the left side? _____

What remains on the right side? _____

What is the solution? _____

TRY IT TOGETHER

Solve each equation. Then check the solution.

4 $k + {}^-3 = 7$

$$\underline{\quad -\square}$$
$$k = \square$$

Check: $k + {}^-3 = 7$

$$\underline{} + {}^-3 \stackrel{?}{=} 7$$
$$\underline{} = 7$$

5 $10.2 = 6.18 + s$

$$\underline{-\square \quad -\square}$$
$$\square = s$$

Check: $10.2 = 6.18 + s$

$$10.2 \stackrel{?}{=} 6.18 + \underline{}$$
$$10.2 = \underline{}$$

6 $y - 29 = 18$

$$\underline{+\square \quad +\square}$$
$$y = \square$$

Check: $y - 29 = 18$

$$\underline{} - 29 \stackrel{?}{=} 18$$
$$\underline{} = 18$$

WORK ON YOUR OWN

HOW TO

Solve One-Step Equations Using Addition and Subtraction

Using Symbols	Using Words
1. $y - 7 = 26$	Get the variable by itself on one side of the equation.
$y - 7 + 7 = 26 + 7$ $y = 33$	If the equation has a variable plus a number, then subtract that number from both sides of the equation.
	If the equation has a variable minus a number, then add that number to both sides of the equation.
2. Check: $y - 7 = 26$ $33 - 7 \stackrel{?}{=} 26$ $26 \stackrel{\checkmark}{=} 26$	To check, substitute the solution for the variable. If both sides of the equation are equal, then the solution is correct.

SKILL BUILDING: NEW AND REVIEW

Solve each equation. Then check the solution.

7 $a - 20 = 50$

8 $b + {}^-17 = {}^-30$

9 $h + 3.4 = 10.3$

10 $6 = 1.5 + x$

11 $j - 1.5 = 3.5$

12 ${}^-6.2 = y + {}^-6.2$

Evaluate each expression.

13 $23 - s$, when $s = {}^-3$

14 $m + 8$, when $m = {}^-12$

15 $k - 40$, when $k = 100$

PROBLEM-SOLVING

Using Reasonableness

The total number of students in Ms. Garcia's class is 35. There are 18 boys in the class. Set up and solve an equation to find the number of girls in the class.

a. **Find:** an equation to find the number of girls in the class

b. **How?** Set up and solve an equation.

c. **Solve.**

Number of girls plus number of boys equals total number of students.

$$g + 18 = 35$$
$$- 18 \quad - 18$$
$$\underline{\qquad} = \underline{\qquad}$$

d. **Is the answer reasonable? Explain.** _____

_____

_____

PROBLEM-SOLVING: NEW AND REVIEW

Solve each problem.

16 The total number of students in Mr. Piper's class is 27. There are 11 girls in the class. Set up and solve an equation to find the number of boys in the class.

17 Sarah was buying sweet potatoes at the store. She had 7.5 pounds of potatoes on the scale. Sarah put two more potatoes on the scale, bringing the total weight to 9 pounds. Solve the equation $7.5 + p = 9$ to find how much the two added potatoes weighed.

18 Luis bought 2 items at the grocery store for a total bill of $14.95. The first item cost $9.25. Solve the equation $b + 9.25 = 14.95$ to find how much the second item cost.

19 Is $(^-3)^4$ the same as $^-(3)^4$? Explain.

CHECK UP

Answer each question.

1 What is the solution of $w + 7 = {}^-23$?

   a. $w = {}^-16$ **b.** $w = 16$

   c. $w = 30$ **d.** $w = {}^-30$

2 What is the solution of $2.9 = b - 4.5$?

   a. $b = 6.4$ **b.** $b = 7.4$

   c. $b = 2.6$ **d.** $b = 1.6$

3 Which two answer choices in problem 1 are the least reasonable? Explain.

_____

_____

_____

4 Stefan collected shells during his vacation. He gave 27 of the shells to his cousin and still had 38 left. Write and solve an equation to find the number of shells Stefan collected during his vacation. Use the variable s. If Mike collected 50 shells, who collected more? Explain.

_____

_____

_____

Solving One-Step Equations Using Multiplication and Division

Name _____ Class _____ Date _____

GET STARTED

 a. $20p$, when $p = {}^-2$

$$20p = 20 \times \underline{\hspace{1cm}}$$

$$= \underline{\hspace{1cm}}$$

b. $\dfrac{t}{7}$, when $t = {}^-63$

$$\dfrac{t}{7} = \dfrac{\underline{\hspace{0.6cm}}}{7}$$

$$= \underline{\hspace{1cm}}$$

c. $\dfrac{a}{2}$, when $a = {}^-6$

$$\dfrac{a}{2} = \dfrac{\underline{\hspace{0.6cm}}}{2}$$

$$= \underline{\hspace{1cm}}$$

$${}^-8x = 56$$
$$\dfrac{{}^-8x}{\underline{\hspace{0.6cm}}} = \dfrac{56}{\underline{\hspace{0.6cm}}}$$
$$x = \underline{\hspace{1cm}}$$

Check:
$${}^-8x = 56$$
$${}^-8 \times \underline{\hspace{1cm}} \overset{?}{=} 56$$
$$\underline{\hspace{1cm}} = 56$$

3
$$\dfrac{1}{8} = \dfrac{m}{3}$$
$$\underline{\hspace{1cm}} \times \dfrac{1}{8} = \dfrac{m}{3} \times \underline{\hspace{1cm}}$$
$$\dfrac{\underline{\hspace{0.6cm}}}{\underline{\hspace{0.6cm}}} = m$$

Check:
$$\dfrac{1}{8} = \dfrac{m}{3}$$
$$\dfrac{1}{8} \overset{?}{=} \dfrac{\underline{\hspace{0.6cm}}}{\underline{\hspace{0.6cm}}} \div 3$$
$$\dfrac{1}{8} \overset{?}{=} \dfrac{\underline{\hspace{0.6cm}}}{\underline{\hspace{0.6cm}}} \times \dfrac{1}{3}$$
$$\dfrac{1}{8} = \dfrac{\underline{\hspace{0.6cm}}}{\underline{\hspace{0.6cm}}} = \dfrac{\underline{\hspace{0.6cm}}}{\underline{\hspace{0.6cm}}}$$

BUILD THE CONCEPT

Look at the equation modeled by the algebra tiles.

What is the equation? _____

How many groups can be created so that there is only one x tile in each group? _____

How many ones tiles are in each group? _____

What is the solution? _____

TRY IT TOGETHER

Solve each equation. Then check the solution.

4 $^-6k = {}^-54$

$$\frac{^-6k}{\boxed{}} = \frac{^-54}{\boxed{}}$$

$$k = \underline{\hphantom{0000}}$$

Check: $^-6k = {}^-54$

$$^-6 \times \underline{\hphantom{000}} \overset{?}{=} {}^-54$$

$$\underline{\hphantom{000}} = {}^-54$$

5

$$\frac{r}{15} = {}^-10$$

$$\underline{\hphantom{000}} \times \frac{r}{15} = {}^-10 \times \underline{\hphantom{000}}$$

$$r = \underline{\hphantom{000}}$$

Check: $\dfrac{r}{15} = {}^-10$

$$\frac{\boxed{}}{15} \overset{?}{=} {}^-10$$

$$\underline{\hphantom{000}} = {}^-10$$

WORK ON YOUR OWN

HOW TO

Solve One-Step Equations Using Multiplication and Division

Using Symbols	Using Words
1. $3t = 15$ $\dfrac{3t}{3} = \dfrac{15}{3}$ $t = 5$	Get the variable by itself on one side of the equation. If the equation has a variable multiplied by a number, then divide both sides of the equation by that number. If the equation has a variable divided by a number, then multiply both sides of the equation by that number.
2. Check: $3t = 15$ $3 \times 5 \overset{?}{=} 15$ $15 \overset{\checkmark}{=} 15$	To check, substitute the solution for the variable. If both sides of the equation are equal, then the solution is correct.

Go to
VmathLive.com

Module Pre-Algebra
Activity Solve Equations: Multiply, Divide 2

Vmath Live

Lesson 5

SKILL BUILDING: NEW AND REVIEW

Solve each equation. Then check the solution.

6 $9a = 630$

7 $\dfrac{w}{^-8} = 21$

8 $\dfrac{q}{8} = \dfrac{1}{4}$

9 $\dfrac{n}{0.3} = 9.9$

10 $1.25 = 0.5s$

11 $^-12t = ^-60$

12 $n + 0.15 = 1.15$

13 $t + ^-36 = 100$

14 $\dfrac{1}{6} = q + \dfrac{1}{6}$

PROBLEM-SOLVING: NEW AND REVIEW

Solve each problem.

15 Maria's age is $\dfrac{1}{3}$ of her father's age. Maria is 18 years old. Solve the equation $\dfrac{a}{3} = 18$ to find Maria's father's age.

16 The expression $\dfrac{n}{36}$ can be used to convert inches to yards. The variable n represents the number of inches. How many yards equal 54 inches?

17 Peggy's 9-page report is $1\dfrac{1}{2}$ times as long as Trudy's report. Solve the equation $1\dfrac{1}{2}t = 9$ to find how many pages Trudy's report is.

18 A diver descends underwater 5 feet each minute. Solve the equation $^-5x = ^-15$ to find how many minutes it takes the diver to reach a depth of 15 feet below sea level.

CHECK UP

Answer each question.

1 What is the solution of the equation $\dfrac{b}{^-4} = 23$?

   a. $b = 92$ **b.** $b = {}^-5.75$

   c. $b = {}^-92$ **d.** $b = 19$

2 What is the solution of the equation $^-17z = 34$?

   a. $z = 51$ **b.** $z = {}^-578$

   c. $z = 2$ **d.** $z = {}^-2$

3 How can the solution for each problem be checked?

_____

_____

_____

Janie solves the problem $\dfrac{m}{3} = 27$ by multiplying both sides of the equation by 3. Why did she use multiplication to solve the problem? What is the solution?

_____

_____

_____

_____

4 Mario is collecting stamps. He can put 9 stamps on each page in his stamp collection. How many pages does he need to display 54 stamps? Write and solve an equation to find the number of pages.

_____

_____

_____

Solving Two-Step Equations

Name _____ Class _____ Date _____

GET STARTED

1 $b + 5 = \quad 12$

$$\underline{\quad -\quad\quad -\quad}$$

$b = $

2 $5c = 125$

$$\frac{5c}{\quad} = \frac{125}{\quad}$$

$c = $

3 $6k + 5 = \quad 23$

$$\underline{\quad -\quad\quad -\quad}$$

$6k = $

$$\frac{6k}{\quad} = \underline{\quad}$$

$k = \underline{\quad}$

Check: $6k + 5 = 23$

$6 \times \underline{\quad} + 5 \overset{?}{=} 23$

$\underline{\quad} + 5 \overset{?}{=} 23$

$\underline{\quad} = 23$

4 $\frac{z}{5} + 7 = \quad 3$

$$\underline{\quad -\quad\quad -\quad}$$

$$\frac{z}{5} = $$

$$\underline{\quad} \times \frac{z}{5} = $$

$$\underline{\quad} \times \underline{\quad} = $$

$z = \underline{\quad}$

Check: $\frac{z}{5} + 7 = 3$

$$\frac{\underline{\quad}}{5} + 7 \overset{?}{=} 3$$

$\underline{\quad} + 7 \overset{?}{=} 3$

$\underline{\quad} = 3$

5 $37 = 5g + 12$

$$\underline{\quad -\quad\quad -\quad}$$

$\underline{\quad} = 5g$

$$\underline{\quad} = \frac{5g}{\quad}$$

$\underline{\quad} = g$

Check: $37 = 5g + 12$

$37 \overset{?}{=} 5 \times \underline{\quad} + 12$

$37 \overset{?}{=} \underline{\quad} + 12$

$37 = \underline{\quad}$

TRY IT TOGETHER

Solve each equation. Then check the solution.

6 $\dfrac{v}{2} - 3 = {}^-8$

$$\underline{ + + }$$

$$\dfrac{v}{2} = \boxed{}$$

$$\boxed{} \times \dfrac{v}{2} = \boxed{} \times \boxed{}$$

$$v = \boxed{}$$

Check: $\dfrac{v}{2} - 3 = {}^-8$

$$\dfrac{\boxed{}}{2} - 3 \overset{?}{=} {}^-8$$

$$\underline{} - 3 \overset{?}{=} {}^-8$$

$$\underline{} = {}^-8$$

7 $9q - 16 = 20$

$$\underline{ + + }$$

$$9q = \boxed{}$$

$$\dfrac{9q}{\boxed{}} = \dfrac{\boxed{}}{\underline{}}$$

$$q = \boxed{}$$

Check: $9q - 16 = 20$

$$9 \times \underline{} - 16 \overset{?}{=} 20$$

$$\underline{} - 16 \overset{?}{=} 20$$

$$\underline{} = 20$$

WORK ON YOUR OWN

Solve Two-Step Equations

HOW TO

Using Symbols	**Using Words**
1. Solve: $\dfrac{y}{7} + 3 = 5$ $\dfrac{y}{7} + 3 - 3 = 5 - 3$ $\dfrac{y}{7} = 2$ $7 \times \dfrac{y}{7} = 2 \times 7$ $y = 14$	Get the variable by itself on one side of the equation.
2. Check: $\dfrac{y}{7} + 3 = 5$ $\dfrac{14}{7} + 3 \overset{?}{=} 5$ $2 + 3 \overset{?}{=} 5$ $5 = 5$	To check, substitute the solution for the variable. If both sides of the equation are equal, then the solution is correct.

SKILL BUILDING: NEW AND REVIEW

Solve each equation. Then check the solution.

8 $7u - 9 = 47$

9 $\dfrac{m}{8} - 10 = {}^-2$

10 $3t + 3 = 3$

11 $0.7 = \dfrac{j}{3.2}$

12 $^-36 = 9h$

13 $2.1 + p = 3.9$

14 $\dfrac{y}{3} - 2 = 9$

15 $5g - 12 = 33$

16 $\dfrac{d}{20} + 6 = 5$

PROBLEM-SOLVING

Using a 4-Step Plan

A plumber charges $20 to make a house call. He then charges $25 for each hour of work. He charged $120 for one job. Solve the equation $25x + 20 = 120$ to find the number of hours he worked.

   a. **Find:** how many hours the plumber worked

   b. **How?** Solve a two-step equation.

   c. **Solve:**

$$25x + 20 = 120$$
$$25x + 20 - 20 = 120 - 20$$
$$25x = 100$$
$$\frac{25x}{25} = \frac{100}{25}$$
$$x = \underline{\hspace{1cm}}$$

The plumber worked _____ hours.

   d. **Check:** _____

_____

Go to
VmathLive.com

Module Pre-Algebra
Activity Solve Two-Step Equations

PROBLEM-SOLVING: NEW AND REVIEW

Solve each problem.

17 An electrician charges $15 to make a house call. He then charges $20 for each hour of work. He charged $95 for one job. Solve the equation $20x + 15 = 95$ to find the number of hours he worked.

18 To take a taxicab from the airport, it costs $5 plus an additional $1.50 for every mile traveled. Tamara paid $20 for a cab ride from the airport to her hotel. Solve the equation $5 + 1.50m = 20$ to find how many miles Tamara traveled in the taxicab.

19 Charlie spent half as long working on the computer as Mary. Charlie spent 40 minutes working on the computer. Solve the equation $\frac{m}{2} = 40$ to find how long Mary spent working on the computer.

20 Lois had $20 in her savings account. For her birthday, she received equal amounts from 3 relatives and now has a total of $50 in her account. Which equation would you use to find how much each relative gave her: $20 - 3x = 50$ or $20 + 3x = 50$? Solve the equation.

CHECK UP

Answer each question.

1 What is the solution of the equation $\frac{a}{13} + 3 = 5$?

   a. $a = 2$ **b.** $a = 104$

   c. $a = 62$ **d.** $a = 26$

2 What is the solution of the equation $8n - 8 = 24$?

   a. $n = 11$ **b.** $n = 32$

   c. $n = 2$ **d.** $n = 4$

3 What value of t would make the equation $\frac{t}{12} - 5 = 2$ true? Explain how to find the value of t. _____

_____

_____

WRITE MATH

4 Fill in the blanks with the correct values from the equation $3x + 4 = 25$ so that it models the word problem.

CRITICAL THINKING

Jena buys a bag of _____ apples. She gives _____ to her mother. The rest of the apples are split equally among herself and her two brothers. Each sibling receives _____ apples.

Solve the equation $3x + 4 = 25$ to find how many apples each sibling receives. _____

Each sibling receives _____ apples.

New Vocabulary
input-output table
function rule
function

Input-Output Tables

Name _____ Class _____ Date _____

GET STARTED

1 **a.** $x + 5$, when $x = {}^-1$

$x + 5 = $ _____ $+ 5$

$= $ _____

b. $x + 5$, when $x = 1$

$x + 5 = $ _____ $+ 5$

$= $ _____

2

In x	Function Rule y = x + 5	Out y
⁻1	$y = {}^-1 + 5 = 4$	4
1	$y = 1 + 5 = 6$	
3	$y = 3 + 5 = $ ____	
5	$y = $ ____ $+ 5 = $ ____	

3

In x	Function Rule y = x − 4	Out y
⁻2	$y = {}^-2 - 4 = {}^-6$	⁻6
0	$y = 0 - 4 = {}^-4$	
2	$y = 2 - 4 = $ ____	
4	$y = $ ____ $-$ ____ $= $ ____	

Scarlett paid $10 to join a stamp collecting club. Each month that she chooses to receive new stamps, she must pay an additional $6. How can she use a function rule to find how much she will spend on the club if she receives stamps for 3 months, 6 months, or 12 months?

Let x represent the number of months that Scarlett will receive stamps.
Let y represent the total amount she will spend.

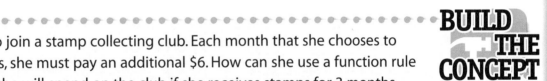

amount Scarlett will spend = cost per month × number of months + cost of joining

y = $6 × x + $ _____

Function Rule: $y = 6x + 10$

Months x	Cost y
3	28
6	____
____	____

Scarlett will pay $28 for 3 months, _____ for 6 months, or _____ for 12 months.

Lesson 7

TRY IT TOGETHER

Complete each input-output table.

4

In x	Function Rule $y = 2x + 5$	Out y
0	$y = \underline{\ \ } \times \underline{\ \ } + \underline{\ \ } = \underline{\ \ }$	
2	$y = \underline{\ \ } \times \underline{\ \ } + \underline{\ \ } = \underline{\ \ }$	
4	$y = \underline{\ \ } \times \underline{\ \ } + \underline{\ \ } = \underline{\ \ }$	
6	$y = \underline{\ \ } \times \underline{\ \ } + \underline{\ \ } = \underline{\ \ }$	

5

In x	Function Rule $y = x \div 2$	Out y
$^-2$	$y = \underline{\ \ } \div \underline{\ \ } = \underline{\ \ }$	
0	$y = \underline{\ \ } \div \underline{\ \ } = \underline{\ \ }$	
2	$y = \underline{\ \ } \div \underline{\ \ } = \underline{\ \ }$	
4	$y = \underline{\ \ } \div \underline{\ \ } = \underline{\ \ }$	

WORK ON YOUR OWN

HOW TO

Complete an Input-Output Table

Using Symbols

In x	Function Rule $y = {^-}2x \times 3$	Out y
$^-1$	$y = {^-}2 \times {^-}1 + 3 = 5$	5

Using Words

For each input value, x:

Substitute the given input value into the function rule for the variable x.

Evaluate the function rule to find the value of y.

Write the output value, y, in the table.

Go to
VmathLive.com

Module Pre-Algebra
Activity Function Rules and Tables

V math Live

Lesson 7

SKILL BUILDING: NEW AND REVIEW

Complete each input-output table.

6

In x	Function Rule $y = {}^-2x$	Out y
⁻1		
0		
1		
2		

7

In x	Function Rule $y = 2x + 1$	Out y
0		
2		
4		
6		

Solve each equation. Then check the solution.

8 $1 = x - 1$

9 $11 = 2x + 1$

PROBLEM-SOLVING: NEW AND REVIEW

Solve each problem.

10   Liz worked a total of 38 hours during the last two weeks. She worked 18.5 hours the first week. Solve the equation $18.5 + t = 38$ to find the number of hours she worked the second week.

11   Hal is 9 years older than Jill. Let x represent Jill's age and y represent Hal's age. The function rule $y = x + 9$ can be used to find Hal's age given Jill's age. How old will Hal be when Jill is 15 years old? Complete the input-output table to find Hal's age when Jill is 15 years old and 20 years old.

In x	Function Rule $y = x + 9$	Out y
10	$y = 10 + 9 = 19$	19
15		
20		

12   A day care charges a flat fee of $90 per week for a school-age child for after-school care. It also adds an extra $8 per day for non-school days. Solve the equation $90 + 8d = 114$ to find how many non-school days there were in one week if a mother was charged $114.

13   A car dealer sells only heavy-duty trucks that have 6 wheels. On any day, there may be a different number of trucks on the lot. Write a function rule that can be used to find the number of wheels on the lot, y, as a function of the number of trucks on the lot, x. Use an input-output table to find the number of wheels on the lot when there are 5 trucks, 8 trucks, or 10 trucks.

In x	Function Rule	Out y
5		
8		
10		

CHECK UP

Answer each question.

1 A function rule is $y = \frac{x}{3}$. What is the value of y if the value of x is 9?

    a. $y = 3$ **b.** $y = {}^-3$

    c. $y = 6$ **d.** $y = 27$

2 A function rule is $y = 3x - 6$. What is the value of y if the value of x is 12?

    a. $y = 18$ **b.** $y = 6$

    c. $y = 42$ **d.** $y = 30$

3 For the function rule $y = {}^-4x$, which input value would result in a greater output value: 5 or 6? Why? _____

_____

_____

_____

WRITE MATH

EXPLAIN IT

Jacob is 4 years older than his sister. He created an input-output table to find how old she will be when he is different ages. He let y represent his sister's age and x represent his own age. Is Jacob's function rule correct? Explain. Are all of Jacob's output values correct? Explain.

_____

_____

_____

_____

_____

_____

_____

_____

_____

In	Function Rule	Out
x	$y = x - 4$	y
15	$y = 15 - 4 = 11$	11
20	$y = 20 - 4 = 16$	16
25	$y = 25 - 4 = 21$	21
30	$y = 30 - 4 = 26$	26
35	$y = 35 - 4 = 32$	32

4 If a function rule is $y = x + 9$, will all input values result in positive output values? Why or why not?_____

_____

_____

_____

CRITICAL THINKING

Function Rules

Name _____ Class _____ Date _____

GET STARTED

In x	Function Rule y = x − 3	Out y
⁻2	y = ⁻2 − 3 = ⁻5	⁻5
⁻1	y = ⁻1 − 3 = _____	
0	y = 0 − 3 = _____	
1	y = _____ − _____ = _____	

x	y
⁻10	⁻2
⁻5	⁻1
5	1
10	2

Function rule:

y = _____

x	y
⁻2	6
⁻1	3
0	0
1	⁻3

Function rule:

y = _____

4

x	y
2	⁻2
4	⁻4
6	⁻6
8	

Function rule:

y = _____ = _____

BUILD THE CONCEPT

Hannah and Mitchell are siblings. The input-output table shows the relationship between their ages at different times in their lives. What is their relationship expressed as a function rule?

Hannah's Age, x	Mitchell's Age, y
3	6
8	11
12	15
15	18

x + 3 = y	or	2x = y
3 + 3 = 6		2 × 3 = 6
8 + 3 = 11		2 × 8 = _____
12 + 3 = _____		
15 + 3 = _____		

Function Rule:

Mitchell's age is Hannah's age plus three.

_____

TRY IT TOGETHER

Write each function rule. Then complete the input-output table.

5

x	y
2	22
4	24
6	26
8	

y = _____

6

x	y
2	⁻3
4	⁻1
6	1
8	

y = _____

7

x	y
⁻3	⁻1
0	0
3	1
6	

y = _____

WORK ON YOUR OWN

HOW TO

Find a Function Rule for an Input-Output Table

Using Symbols	Using Words
1. <table><tr><th>x</th><th>y</th></tr><tr><td>⁻1</td><td>⁻4</td></tr><tr><td>0</td><td>⁻3</td></tr><tr><td>1</td><td>⁻2</td></tr><tr><td>2</td><td>⁻1</td></tr></table> input ⁻1, output ⁻4	Compare an input value with its output value.
2. $⁻1 - 3 = ⁻4$ or $⁻1 \times 4 = ⁻4$	Determine what was done to the input value, x, to get the output value, y.
3. $0 - 3 = ⁻3$ $0 \times 4 \neq ⁻3$ $1 - 3 = ⁻2$ $2 - 3 = ⁻1$	Verify that the same rule works for every input-output pair.
4. $y = x - 3$	Write the function rule.

SKILL BUILDING: NEW AND REVIEW

Write each function rule. Then complete the input-output table.

8

x	y
‾2	‾9
‾1	‾8
1	‾6
2	

$y =$ _____

9

x	y
‾2	10
‾1	5
1	‾5
2	

$y =$ _____

10

x	y
‾4	‾2
‾2	‾1
0	0
2	

$y =$ _____

Complete each input-output table.

11

In x	Function Rule $y = 2x - 1$	Out y
0		
1		
2		
3		

12

In x	Function Rule $y = \dfrac{x}{10} + 5$	Out y
0		
10		
20		
30		

PROBLEM-SOLVING

Using a Table

The table shows how much it costs to see a movie in a theater.
Write a function rule for the table.

a. **Find:** a function rule for the table

b. **How?** Use the information in the table to find a rule that works for all input-output pairs.

c. **Solve.** Input $x = 2$ Output $y =$ _____

The function rule could be $y = 9$.

Check the remaining pairs.

_____ × _____ = _____   _____ × _____ = _____   _____ × _____ = _____

d. **Is the answer reasonable? Explain.** _____

_____

_____

People, x	Cost ($), y
2	18
4	36
5	45
8	72

Lesson 8

V math LIVE

Go to
VmathLive.com

Module Pre-Algebra
Activity Find the Function Rule

PROBLEM-SOLVING: NEW AND REVIEW

Solve each problem using the table.

Animals, x	Minutes, y
3	21
5	35
7	49
?	63

13 The table shows how long it takes Toby to make origami animals. Write a function rule for the table.

14 How many origami animals can Toby make in 63 minutes? Explain.

15 Use the function rule from problem 13 to find how long it will take Toby to make 13 animals.

16 Use the function rule from problem 13 to find how long it will take Toby to make 20 animals.

CHECK UP

Answer each question.

1 What is the function rule for the table?

a. $y = 2x$

b. $y = x + 18$

c. $y = {}^-2x$

d. $y = \dfrac{x}{{}^-2}$

x	y
⁻6	12
⁻5	10
0	0
3	⁻6

2 What is the function rule for the table?

a. $y = {}^-3x$

b. $y = x - 20$

c. $y = \dfrac{x}{{}^-3}$

d. $y = x + 20$

x	y
⁻15	5
3	⁻1
12	⁻4
24	⁻8

3 Which answer choices in problem 2 are the least reasonable? Explain.

_____

_____

_____

4 An input-output table does not show a function rule. Brian notices that each output value can be multiplied by 2 to arrive at the corresponding input value. What is the function rule? Explain.

_____

_____

_____

_____

New Vocabulary
sequence
term

Problem-Solving: Using a Table

Name _____ Class _____ Date _____

GET STARTED

1

x	y
5	10
7	14
9	18

Function rule:

y = _____

2

x	y
0	1
2	3
4	5

Function rule:

y = _____

3 At a craft store, 5 yards of ribbon cost $6, 7 yards cost $8.40, and 9 yards cost $10.80. How many yards of ribbon can be bought for $13.20?

a. **Find:** _____

b. **How?** _____

_____

c. **Solve.**

Yards, x	Cost, y
5	6

y = _____

_____ = _____

_____ = _____

_____ = x

Function rule: _____

_____ yards of ribbon can be bought for $13.20.

d. **Is the answer correct? Explain.** _____

_____

TRY IT TOGETHER

Solve the problem.

4 Kendra starts to knit a scarf. After 8 minutes, the scarf is 2 inches long. After 12 minutes, it is 3 inches long, and after 16 minutes, it is 4 inches long. At this rate, how long will Kendra's scarf be after 20 minutes?

a. **Find:** _____

b. **How?** _____

_____

c. **Solve.**

Minutes, x	Inches, y
8	2

Function rule:

_____

$y = \dfrac{}{} = \dfrac{}{} = $ _____

The scarf will be _____ long after 20 minutes.

d. **Is the answer reasonable? Explain.** _____

_____

WORK ON YOUR OWN

HOW TO

Solve a Problem by Using a Table

A printer prints 16 pages in 2 minutes, 32 pages in 4 minutes, and 48 pages in 6 minutes. How long does it take to print 120 pages?

1. **Find:** the amount of time the printer takes to print 120 pages

2. **How?** Make an input-output table, find a function rule, then use the rule to solve the problem.

Number of Minutes, x	Number of Pages, y
2	16
4	32
6	48

3. **Solve.**
   The function rule is $y = 8x$.
   Substitute for y in the function rule: $y = 8x$
   $$120 = 8x$$
   $$15 = x$$
   It takes 15 minutes to print 120 pages.

4. **Is the answer reasonable? Explain.** Yes, $8 \times 15 = 120$, which is the original number of pages.

SKILL BUILDING: NEW AND REVIEW

Solve each problem.

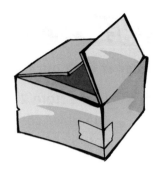

5 Kelly can pack 100 magazines in 4 boxes, 150 magazines in 6 boxes, and 200 magazines in 8 boxes. How many magazines can she pack in 12 boxes?

6 Nico has $34 in his lunch account at school, and Juan has $31. When Nico has $28 in his account, Juan has $25. When Nico has $22 in his lunch account, Juan has $19. How much money will be in Juan's lunch account when Nico's lunch account is $18?

7 The number of minutes Jaime spends delivering newspapers can be found using the expression $14 + 2c$, where c represents the number of newspapers he delivers. If Jaime delivers 28 newspapers, how many minutes will it take him?

Write each function rule. Then complete the input-output table.

8

x	y
⁻2	3
⁻1	4
1	6
2	

$y =$ _____

9

x	y
⁻2	12
⁻1	6
1	⁻6
2	

$y =$ _____

10

x	y
⁻2	⁻5
⁻1	⁻4
1	⁻2
2	

$y =$ _____

PROBLEM-SOLVING: NEW AND REVIEW

Solve each problem.

11 A painter is buying paint. Two gallons of paint cost $28, 5 gallons of paint cost $70, and 6 gallons of paint cost $84. How many gallons of paint can the painter buy with $126?

12 Natalie painted 3 more than 2 times the number of beads that Sierra painted. Natalie painted 15 beads. Solve the equation $15 = 2s + 3$ to find s, the number of beads Sierra painted.

13 Joann needs 14 pieces of candy for 7 children, 18 pieces of candy for 9 children, and 22 pieces of candy for 11 children. She calculated that she would need 24 pieces of candy for 14 children. Is she correct? Explain.

CHECK UP

Answer each question.

1 At the store, 2 marbles cost $0.50, 6 marbles cost $1.50, and 10 marbles cost $2.50. How much will 9 marbles cost?

    a. $4.50   **b.** $0.25

    c. $2.25   **d.** $2.50

2 When Juan was 13 years old, his brother was 9 years old. When Juan was 15 years old, his brother was 11 years old. This year, Juan is 17 years old. How old is Juan's brother?

    a. 21 years old   **b.** 12 years old

    c. 12 years old   **d.** 13 years old

3 Which answer choice in problem 1 is the least reasonable? Explain.

WRITE MATH

_____

_____

_____

EXPLAIN IT

On a recent trip, Mr. Harris's car used 2 gallons of gasoline to go 60 miles. When he had traveled 120 miles, 4 gallons of gasoline were used. When he had traveled 180 miles, 6 gallons of gasoline were used.

What is the first step to find how far Mr. Harris traveled if 10 gallons of gasoline were used? Explain your answer, then solve.

_____

_____

_____

_____

4 A function rule is given by $y = {}^-4x$. What happens to the output value if the input value increases? Use an input-output table to show the answer.

_____

_____

x	y
1	
2	
4	
8	

CRITICAL THINKING

Guided Discovery

Points in the Coordinate Plane—
Activity A

Name _____ Class _____ Date _____

Gizmos Log In Instructions
When you are told, log in to the Gizmos as follows:
- Log in to VmathLive using your Username and Password.
- Select the Gizmos tab.
- Click on the Points in the Coordinate Plane—Activity A Gizmo link.

GET READY

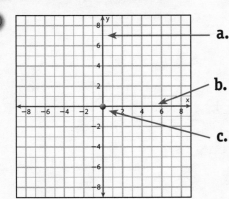

a. _____

b. _____

c. _____

DISCOVER

2 Drag a point onto the coordinate plane.

The ordered pair for the point is (_____ , _____).

a. Drag the slider for *x* back and forth.

The first coordinate is the _____-coordinate.

As the value of *x* changes, the point moves _____.

Drag the slider for *x* so that *x* is positive.

The ordered pair for the point is (_____ , _____).

The point is _____ the *y*-axis.

The point is _____ units from the *y*-axis.

Drag the slider for *x* so that *x* is negative.

The ordered pair for the point is (_____ , _____).

The point is _____ the *y*-axis.

The point is _____ units from the *y*-axis.

b. Drag the slider for *y* back and forth.

The second coordinate is the _____-coordinate.

As the value of *y* changes, the point moves _____.

Drag the slider for *y* so that *y* is positive.

The ordered pair for the point is (_____ , _____).

The point is _____ the *x*-axis.

The point is _____ units from the *x*-axis.

Drag the slider for *y* so that *y* is negative.

The ordered pair for the point is (_____ , _____).

The point is _____ the *x*-axis.

The point is _____ units from the *x*-axis.

3 **a.** Check Show quadrant labels.

Drag a point onto the coordinate plane so that it is 3 units to the right of the *y*-axis and 4 units above the *x*-axis.

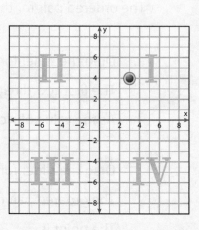

The ordered pair for the point is (_____ , _____).

The *x*-coordinate is _____.

The *y*-coordinate is _____.

The point is in Quadrant _____.

b. Drag the point so that it is 6 units to the left of the *y*-axis and 2 units above the *x*-axis.

The ordered pair for the point is (_____ , _____).

The *x*-coordinate is _____.
The *y*-coordinate is _____.
The point is in Quadrant _____.

c. Drag the point so that it is 1 unit to the left of the *y*-axis and 5 units below the *x*-axis.

The ordered pair for the point is (_____ , _____).

The *x*-coordinate is _____.
The *y*-coordinate is _____.
The point is in Quadrant _____.

d. Drag the point so that it is 4 units to the right of the *y*-axis and 7 units below the *x*-axis.

The ordered pair for the point is (_____ , _____).

The *x*-coordinate is _____.
The *y*-coordinate is _____.
The point is in Quadrant _____.

Drag all four points onto the coordinate plane so that they do not lie on the *x*-axis or the *y*-axis. Use the slider for *x* to change all four *x*-coordinates to 0. What do the points have in common?

_____

Drag all four points in the coordinate plane so that they do not lie on the *x*-axis or the *y*-axis. Use the slider for *y* to change all four *y*-coordinates to 0. What do the points have in common?

_____

EXPLORE MORE

Use the Gizmo to graph each point. Describe the location of the point with respect to the *x*-axis and the *y*-axis.

4   (4, ⁻3)

5   (⁻5, 7)

New Vocabulary
ordered pair
coordinate plane
x-axis
y-axis
origin
quadrants

Lesson 10

Coordinate Plane

Name _____ Class _____ Date _____

GET STARTED

1 **a.** ^-2x, when $x = ^-1$

$^-2x =$ _____

$=$ _____

b. ^-2x, when $x = 1$

$^-2x =$ _____

$=$ _____

2

x	y	(x, y)
⁻1	2	
1	⁻2	

3 $(^-1, 2)$

Quadrant _____

4 $(1, ^-2)$

Quadrant _____

5 Point C

a. Quadrant _____

b. _____

6 Point D

a. Quadrant _____

b. _____

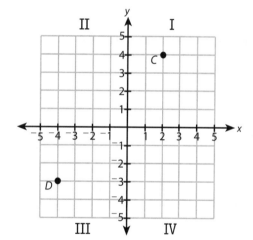

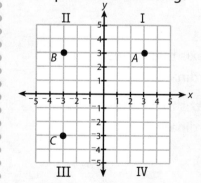

Delphine wants to label the corners of a square on a coordinate plane. What point is she missing?

Point	Quadrant	Ordered Pair
A	I	(3, 3)
B	II	(⁻3, ___)
C		
D		

BUILD THE CONCEPT

To complete the square, the missing point is _____.

TRY IT TOGETHER

Graph each point on the coordinate plane.

7 E(⁻4, 0)

8 F(3, ⁻2)

Write the ordered pair for each point.

9 G _____

10 H _____

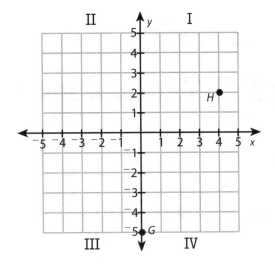

WORK ON YOUR OWN

Graph Points in a Coordinate Plane

Using Symbols	Using Words
Graph Point A at (⁻3, 4). 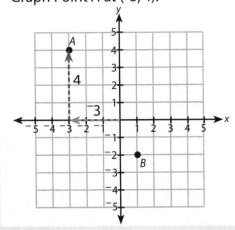	Start at the origin.
	Move x units left or right from the origin. Move right for positive x-coordinates and left for negative x-coordinates.
	Move y units up or down from the x-axis. Move up for positive y-coordinates and down for negative y-coordinates.
	Graph and label the point.

Write an Ordered Pair for a Point on a Coordinate Plane

Using Symbols	Using Words
1. Write the ordered pair for Point B. value on x-axis: _____	Locate the value on the x-axis that corresponds with the point. This is the x-coordinate.
2. value on y-axis: _____	Locate the value on the y-axis that corresponds with the point. This is the y-coordinate.
3. _____	Write the ordered pair (x, y).

SKILL BUILDING: NEW AND REVIEW

Use the coordinate plane for problems 11–18. Write the ordered pair for each point.

11 R _____

12 S _____

13 T _____

14 U _____

Graph each point on the coordinate plane.

15 W($^-$2, $^-$2)

16 X(4, $^-$4)

17 Y(5, 2)

18 Z(3, 0)

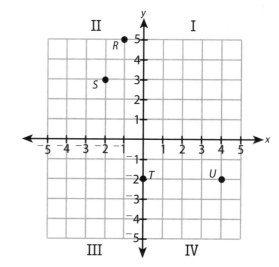

Complete the table.

19

In x	Function Rule $y = \dfrac{x}{3}$	Out y	(x, y)
$^-$3			
0			
3			

PROBLEM-SOLVING

Using Guess and Check

Which two points have the same x-value on the coordinate plane shown? Explain.

a. **Find:** the two points with the same x-coordinate

b. **How?** Guess two points and check their ordered pairs.

c. **Solve.**

First guess: Points C and B → C _____ B _____

Are the x-coordinates the same? _____

Second guess: Points B and A → B _____ A _____

Are the x-coordinates the same? _____

d. **Is the answer reasonable? Explain.** _____

_____

Lesson 10

Vmath**LIVE**

Go to
VmathLive.com

Module Pre-Algebra
Activity Coordinate Graphs

PROBLEM-SOLVING:
NEW AND REVIEW

Solve each problem. Use the coordinate plane for problems 20 and 21.

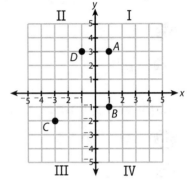

20 Which two points have the same *y*-coordinate? Explain.

21 Write the ordered pair for point *C*.

22 Complete the input-output table.

In x	Function Rule y = x − 2	Out y	(x, y)
⁻2			
⁻1			
1			
2			

CHECK UP

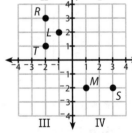

Answer each question.

1 What are the coordinates of point *S*?

   a. (2, ⁻3)   **b.** (⁻3, 2)

   c. (⁻2, 3)   **d.** (3, ⁻2)

2 Which point has the ordered pair (1, ⁻2)?

   a. *L*   **b.** *R*

   c. *M*   **d.** *T*

3 How does knowing the quadrants help eliminate answer choices to problem 1? _____

_____

_____

WRITE MATH

4 A teacher put her pencil on the origin, then moved five places left and drew a point. Ben says the ordered pair for this point is (0, ⁻5). Jeff says the ordered pair for the point is (⁻5, 0) Who is right? Explain.

CRITICAL THINKING

_____

_____

_____

_____

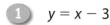
Graphing Linear Equations

Name _____ Class _____ Date _____

GET STARTED

1 $y = x - 3$

x	y = x − 3	y	(x, y)
⁻1	y = ⁻1 − 3	⁻4	(⁻1, ⁻4)
0			
1			

2

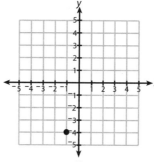

3 $y = {}^-2x$

x	y = ⁻2x	y	(x, y)
⁻2	y = ⁻2 × ⁻2	4	
0			
2			

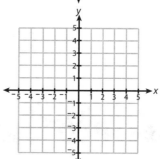

BUILD THE CONCEPT

Lauren is 3 years older than her cousin Maja. Over time, their ages change, but the difference in age between the two girls does not. How can this relationship be shown graphically?

Let x represent Maja's age. Let y represent _____.

The equation for this function is y = _____.

Use the x- and y-values in the input-output table to graph the function rule.

x, Maja's Age	y = _____	y, Lauren's Age	(x, y)
0	y = 0 + 3	3	(0, 3)
1	y = _____	_____	(1, _____)
2	y = _____	_____	(_____, _____)

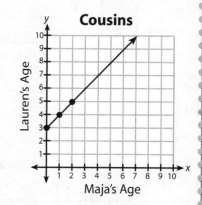

The relationship between Lauren's and Maja's ages remains constant. Lauren will always be 3 years older than Maja. This function rule is called a _____ equation because its graph is a straight line.

TRY IT TOGETHER

Complete each table. Then graph the linear equation.

4 $y = {}^-1x + 1$

x	$y = {}^-1x + 1$	y	(x, y)
$^-4$	$y = {}^-1 \times {}^-4 + 1$		
0	$y = {}^-1 \times 0 + 1$		
4			

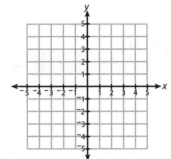

5 $y = \dfrac{x}{4}$

x	$y = \dfrac{x}{4}$	y	(x, y)
$^-4$			
0			
4			

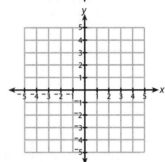

WORK ON YOUR OWN

Graph a Linear Equation

HOW TO

Using Symbols	Using Words
1. $y = x - 2$ 	x	$y = x - 2$	y	(x, y)	 	$^-1$	$y = {}^-1 - 2$	$^-3$	$(^-1, {}^-3)$	 	0	$y = 0 - 2$	$^-2$	$(0, {}^-2)$	 	1	$y = 1 - 2$	$^-1$	$(1, {}^-1)$		Complete the input-output table.
2. $(^-1, {}^-3), (0, {}^-2), (1, {}^-1)$	Use the table to get a set of ordered pairs.
3. 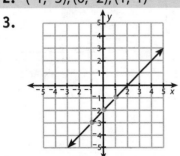	Graph the ordered pairs on a coordinate plane. Draw a line through the points.

Go to
VmathLive.com

Module Pre-Algebra
Activity Graphing from a Table of Values 2

Vmath LIVE

Lesson 11

SKILL BUILDING:
NEW AND REVIEW

Complete each table. Then graph the linear equation.

6 $y = x - 4$

x	y = x − 4	y	(x, y)
⁻1			
0			
1			

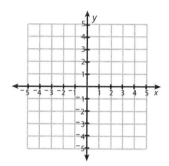

7 $y = 2x - 1$

x	y = 2x − 1	y	(x, y)
⁻1			
0			
1			

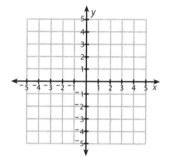

Use the table to answer problems 8 and 9.

8   Write the input-output values in the table as ordered pairs.

9   What is the function rule for the input-output table?

x	y
⁻9	3
⁻6	2
⁻3	1
12	⁻4

PROBLEM-SOLVING:
NEW AND REVIEW

Solve each problem.

10   The table shows some possible values for the number of packs of trading cards, *x*, and the number of cards, *y*, in the packs. What is the function rule for this input-output table?

x	y
1	8
2	16
3	24

11   Write the input-output values in the table as ordered pairs.

12   Describe what this function rule would look like when graphed.

13   Using the function rule from problem 10, what would be the ordered pair with an *x*-coordinate of 4?

CHECK UP

Answer each question.

1 The graph of the linear equation $y = 3x - 2$ is shown. Which of the following points is not on the line?

a. $(^-2, 0)$ **b.** $(^-1, ^-5)$

c. $(1, 1)$ **d.** $(2, 4)$

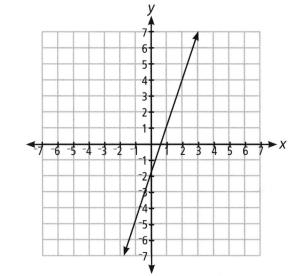

2 For the linear equation in problem 1, what is the value of y when $x = 3$? Write the ordered pair.

3 How can the answer be checked in problem 2?

_____

_____

WRITE MATH

EXPLAIN IT

Three points on the graph of a linear equation are shown. Name another point that is on the graph of this linear equation. Explain why this point must be on the graph.

_____

_____

_____

_____

4 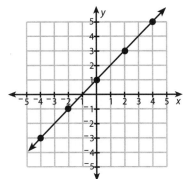 Look at the graph of the linear equation. List the ordered pairs for the five points shown. How does the y-coordinate relate to the x-coordinate in each pair of numbers? Use this relationship to write the function rule in the form $y = $ _____.

ALGEBRAIC THINKING
$\square \times 5$

_____

_____

_____

_____

Finding Slope

Name _____ Class _____ Date _____

GET STARTED

1

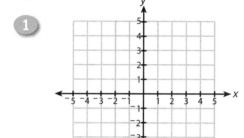

Graph (⁻3, ⁻1) and (3, 1).

2

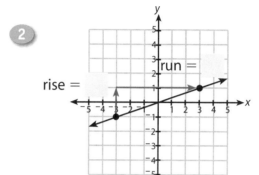

a. slope $= \dfrac{rise}{run} = \underline{\quad} = \underline{\quad}$

b. _____ slope

3

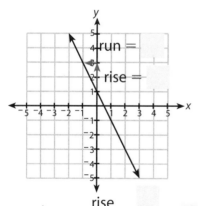

a. slope $= \dfrac{rise}{run} = \underline{\quad} =$

b. _____ slope

4

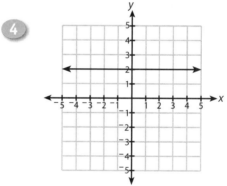

_____ slope

BUILD THE CONCEPT

The lines in the graph represent the flight paths of three model airplanes.

Label each line based on the descriptions.

Plane A: The airplane rises 30 feet for every 100 feet measured along the ground.

Plane B: The airplane descends, or falls, 30 feet for every 100 feet measured along the ground.

Plane C: The airplane neither rises nor falls.

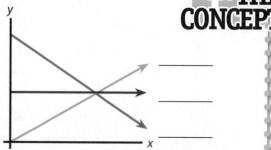

![TRY IT TOGETHER]

Tell whether the slope of each line is positive, negative, or zero. Then find the slope.

5

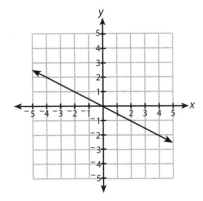

a. _____ slope

b. slope = $\dfrac{\text{rise}}{\text{run}}$ = ⬜/⬜ = ⬜/⬜

6

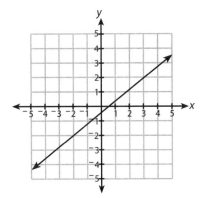

a. _____ slope

b. slope = $\dfrac{\text{rise}}{\text{run}}$ = ⬜/⬜

![WORK ON YOUR OWN]

HOW TO

Find the Slope of a Line

Using Symbols	Using Words
1. (⁻3, 3) and (3, 1)	Identify two points on the line.
2. rise = down 2 → ⁻2	Find the rise between the two points. Rise is positive when moving up and negative when moving down.
3. run = right 6 → 6	Find the run between the two points. Run is positive when moving to the right and negative when moving to the left.
4. slope = $\dfrac{\text{rise}}{\text{run}}$ = $\dfrac{^-2}{6}$ = $\dfrac{^-1}{3}$	Write the ratio of the rise to the run. Simplify the ratio if possible.

SKILL BUILDING: NEW AND REVIEW

Find the slope of each line and tell whether the slope is positive, negative, or zero.

 7

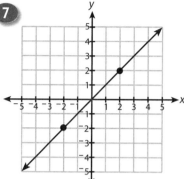

8

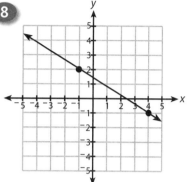

Graph each linear equation and find the slope of each line.

9 $y = {}^-2x + 2$

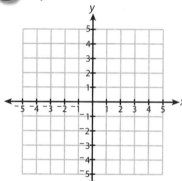

10 $y = 3x + 3$

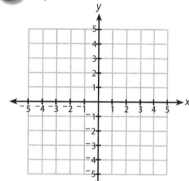

• **PROBLEM-**

Using Guess and Check

SOLVING

Looking at the coordinate graph, which line has a slope of $\frac{1}{2}$?

a. Find: the line that has a slope of $\frac{1}{2}$

b. How? Guess which line it is and find its slope.

c. Solve.

Line *C:* Slope $= \frac{2}{1} = $ _____

Line *D:* Slope $= \dfrac{}{}$

Line _____ has a slope of $\frac{1}{2}$.

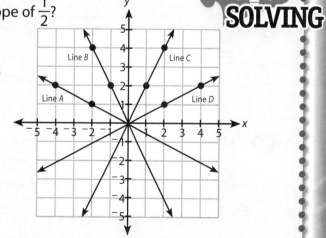

d. Is the answer reasonable? Explain. _____

_____

_____

_____

Lesson 12

V^math LIVE

Go to
VmathLive.com

Module Pre-Algebra
Activity Slope of a Line

PROBLEM-SOLVING: NEW AND REVIEW

Solve each problem.

11 On the Problem-Solving coordinate plane on page 53, which line has a slope of ⁻2?

12 At Hair Now, Sheila can buy 1 headband for $3, 2 headbands for $6, and 3 headbands for $9. Use the information to complete the input-output table and write a function rule for the table.

x	y
1	
2	
3	

13 Find the slope of the line graphed on the coordinate plane.

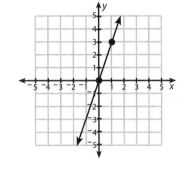

CHECK UP

Answer each question.

1 What is the slope of the line through the points (⁻3, 1) and (3, 1)?

a. 1

b. ⁻1

c. 0

d. 6

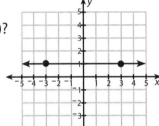

2 What is the slope of this line?

a. $\frac{^-2}{5}$

b. $\frac{^-5}{2}$

c. $\frac{5}{6}$

d. $\frac{5}{2}$

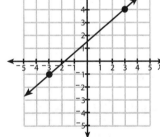

3 Which two answer choices in problem 2 can be automatically eliminated? Explain. _____

_____

WRITE MATH

4 Mariela found the slope of this line by counting from (1, ⁻1) to (3, 3). She got a slope of $\frac{4}{2}$. Lamont found the slope by counting from (3, 3) to (1, ⁻1). He got a slope of $\frac{^-4}{^-2}$. Explain why both are correct.

CRITICAL THINKING

_____

_____

_____

_____

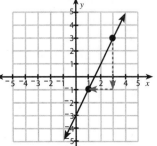

Finding Factors with Area Models

Name _____ Class _____ Date _____

GET READY

1
a. $1 \times$ _____ $= 18$

b. $2 \times$ _____ $= 18$

c. $3 \times$ _____ $= 18$

d. Factors of 18: _____

2
a. $1 \times$ _____ $= 5$

b. Factors of 5: _____

DISCOVER

3
$1 \times$ _____ $= 10$

$2 \times$ _____ $= 10$

Factors of 10: _____

_____ is a prime number.

_____ is a prime number.

Drag the Number to be factored slider to 10.

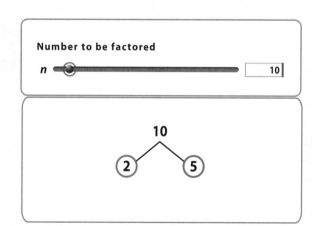

Number to be factored

n 10

The prime factorization of 10 is _____ $\times$ _____.

4   1 × _____ = 20   Factors of 20: _____

2 × _____ = 20

4 × _____ = 20

Drag the Number to be factored slider to 20.

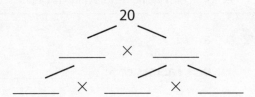

The prime factorization of 20 is _____ × _____ × _____ = _____ × _____ .

5   1 × _____ = 24   Factors of 24: _____

2 × _____ = 24

3 × _____ = 24

4 × _____ = 24

Drag the Number to be factored slider to 24.

Drag the tile bar at the right of the slider one tile to the right.

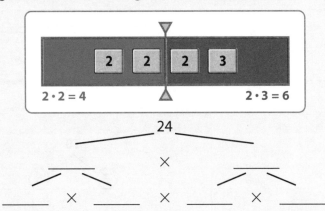

The prime factorization of 24 is

_____ × _____ × _____ × _____ = _____ × _____ .

DISCOVER BOX

Does the choice of the first two factors of a number in a factor tree matter? Explain.

_____

_____

_____

EXPLORE MORE

Use the Gizmo to answer each question.

6 Write the prime factorization of 18. Draw a diagram of the factor tree.

7 Write the prime factorization of 30. Draw a diagram of the factor tree.

Prime Factorization

Name _____ Class _____ Date _____

GET STARTED

 a. 1 × _____ = 24

b. 2 × _____ = 24

c. 3 × _____ = 24

d. 4 × _____ = 24

Factors of 24: _____

 a. 24 _____

b. 13 _____

c. 256 _____

12 = _____

= _____

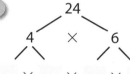

24 = _____

= _____

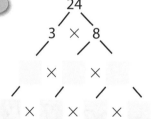

24 = _____

= _____

BUILD THE CONCEPT

The number 42 is factored using three different factor pairs to start the factor tree.

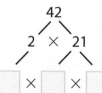

No matter which factor pair is used, the result is the same.

What is the prime factorization of 42? _____ × _____ × _____

TRY IT TOGETHER

Write the prime factorization of each number using exponents.

6

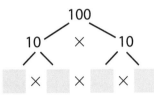

100 = _____ = _____

7

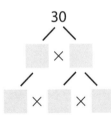

30 = _____

WORK ON YOUR OWN

HOW TO

Find the Prime Factorization of a Whole Number

Using Symbols	Using Words
1. 76 2 × 38 2 × 19 × 2	Choose one pair of factors for the given number. Continue factoring until only prime factors remain.
2. $76 = 2^2 \times 19$	Write the prime factorization from least to greatest, using exponents if possible.

Go to
VmathLive.com

Module Pre-Algebra
Activity Prime Factorization: Exponents

Vmath_{LIVE}

Lesson 13

SKILL BUILDING:
NEW AND REVIEW

Write the prime factorization of each number using exponents.

8 54

9 80

10 135

11 84

12 96

13 160

Determine if each number is prime or composite. If it is composite, list its factors.

14 48

15 53

16 51

PROBLEM-SOLVING:
NEW AND REVIEW

Solve each problem.

17 The prime factorization of a number is $2 \times 3^2 \times 5$. What is the number?

18 A restaurant manager orders boxes of straws. Each box contains 250 straws. How many straws will he have if he orders 1, 2, 3, or 4 boxes of straws?

19 Luis has written the prime factorization of a number as $2^3 \times 7$. What is the sum of Luis's number and 17?

20 Michelle uses the factors 8 and 9 to begin a factor tree for 72. She writes $2^3 \times 3^2$ as the prime factorization of 72. Show how Michelle can use the factor pair 6×12 to check the prime factorization of 72.

CHECK UP

Answer each question.

1 What is the prime factorization of 48?

    a. 2×24 **b.** 2×3

    c. 6×8 **d.** $2^4 \times 3$

2 The number of parking spaces on a certain lot is given by the expression $2^2 \times 3 \times 5 \times 7$. Determine the value of the expression for the number of parking spaces in the parking lot.

    a. 60 spaces   **b.** 105 spaces

    c. 210 spaces   **d.** 420 spaces

3 Which two answer choices in problem 1 can be eliminated based on the factors listed? Explain. _____

_____

_____

WRITE MATH

EXPLAIN IT

Deb listed all the factor pairs of 36: $1 \times 36, 2 \times 18, 3 \times 12, 4 \times 9, 6 \times 6$. She said that based on this information, she could find the prime factorization of 36 in 4 different ways. Is she correct? Explain. What is the prime factorization of 36?

_____

_____

_____

_____

4 In the prime factorization of 60 shown, what is missing? Explain.

$2^2 \times \boxed{} \times 5.$ _____

_____

_____

_____

ALGEBRAIC THINKING

$\square \times 5$

Powers of Ten
and Scientific Notation

Name _____ Class _____ Date _____

GET STARTED

1　**a.**　$10^2 = 10 \times 10 =$ _____

　　b.　$10^3 =$ _____ $\times$ _____ $\times$ _____ $=$ _____

　　c.　$10^6 =$ _____ $\times$ _____ $\times$ _____ $\times$ _____ $\times$ _____ $\times$ _____ $=$ _____

2

8.0035 first factor	**×**	**10^4** second factor
a number greater than or equal to 1 and less than 10	×	power of 10

3　$80,000 =$ _____ $\times 10$　　　　**4**　$3,090 =$ _____ $\times 10$

5　$6.912 \times 10^5 =$ _____　　**6**　$4 \times 10^6 =$ _____

　　6.912　　　　　　　　　　　　　　　$4.$

BUILD THE CONCEPT

To write a large number such as 158,000,000,000 in scientific notation, consider how many times 1.58 has to be multiplied by 10 to get 158,000,000,000.

$1.58 \times 10 = 15.8$
$15.8 \times 10 = 158.$
$158 \times 10 = 1,580$
$1,580 \times 10 = 15,800$
$15,800 \times 10 = 158,000$
$158,000 \times 10 = 1,580,000$
$1,580,000 \times 10 = 15,800,000$
$15,800,000 \times 10 = 158,000,000$
$158,000,000 \times 10 = 1,580,000,000$
$1,580,000,000 \times 10 = 15,800,000,000$
$15,800,000,000 \times 10 = 158,000,000,000$

$1.58 \times$ _____ tens $= 158,000,000,000$

158,000,000,000 written in scientific notation is _____.

TRY IT TOGETHER

Write each number in scientific notation.

7 600,000 = _____

8 403,000,000 = _____

Write each number in standard form.

9 7×10^3 = _____

7.

10 2.084×10^6 = _____

2.084

WORK ON YOUR OWN

HOW TO

Write a Standard Form Number in Scientific Notation

Using Symbols	Using Words
1. $3,820,000,000 \rightarrow$ 3.82	Move the decimal point in the number to form a number greater than or equal to 1 and less than 10, dropping all trailing 0s. This is the first factor.
2. 9 places $\rightarrow 10^9$ $3,820,000,000 = 3.82 \times 10^9$	Count the number of places the decimal point moved. This is the exponent of the power of 10.

Write a Scientific Notation Number in Standard Form

Using Symbols	Using Words
1. $2.7 \times 10^5 \rightarrow$ exponent is 5	Identify the exponent of the power of 10. This is the number of places the decimal point has to be moved.
2. 2.70000	Locate the decimal point in the number and move the decimal point to the right the number of places indicated by the exponent.
3. $2.7 \times 10^5 = 270,000$	Write 0s as placeholders if needed.

SKILL BUILDING: NEW AND REVIEW

Write each number in scientific notation.

11 5,602,000

12 345,000

13 29,900

14 4,000,000

15 6,040

16 70,100,000

Write each number in standard form.

17 6.7×10^5

18 8.99×10^7

19 1.01×10^3

20 3.02×10^2

21 6.345×10^9

22 2.45×10^6

Find the value of each exponential expression.

23 3^4

24 7^3

25 25^2

PROBLEM-SOLVING

Using a Problem-Solving Plan

In a laboratory, a scientist found that there were about 7.3×10^9 cells in Specimen A and 42,000,000,000 cells in Specimen B. Which specimen has more cells?

a. **Find:** the specimen with the greater number of cells

b. **How?** Change the number of cells to the same form and compare.

c. **Solve.**

Specimen A: 7.3×10^9 = _____

Specimen B: 42,000,000,000

Compare. 7,300,000,000 ☐ 42,000,000,000

Specimen _____ has more cells.

d. **Is the answer reasonable? Explain.** _____

_____

_____

PROBLEM-SOLVING: NEW AND REVIEW

Solve each problem.

26 The area of the Arctic Ocean is about 1.41×10^7 square kilometers. The area of the Atlantic Ocean is about 82,400,000 square kilometers. Which ocean has the greater area?

27 Light travels through space at a rate of about 2.998×10^8 meters per second. What is this number written in standard form?

28 During his experiment, Frank needed to record results every 8.5 minutes. If the experiment ran for 93.5 minutes, how many times did he record results?

CHECK UP

Answer each question.

1 What is 36,200,000 written in scientific notation?

   a. 3.62×10^5 **b.** 0.362×10^8

   c. 3.62×10^7 **d.** 3.62×10^8

2 Earth is about 1.5×10^8 kilometers from the Sun. How is this number written in standard form?

   a. 1,500,000 km

   b. 15,000,000 km

   c. 150,000,000 km

   d. 1,500,000, 000 km

3 Which answer choice in problem 1 is the least reasonable? Explain.

_____

_____

_____

4 A homework problem asks students to compare A and B, where $A = 8 \times 10^5$ and $B = 7 \times 10^6$. Jack says A is larger than B because the first factor in A, 8, is greater than the first factor in B, 7. Anna says B is larger than A because the second factor in B, 10^6, is greater than the second factor in A, 10^5. Who is correct? Explain. _____

_____

_____

_____

_____

_____

New Vocabulary
inequality

Inequalities

Name _____ Class _____ Date _____

GET STARTED

1

<	≤		
is less than	is less than or equal to	is greater than	is greater than or equal to

2 **a.** $2 < 7$ true   false

     b. $4 > 9$ true   false

3 **a.** y is less than 3

         y 3

     c. m is less than or equal to 0

         m 0

     b. $^-1$ is greater than a

         $^-1$ a

     d. $2\frac{1}{2}$ is greater than or equal to k

         $2\frac{1}{2}$ k

4 **a.** p is at most 5

     _____   _____

     b. w is at least 4.1

     _____   _____

5 **a.** $x > 7$ or 7 x

     b. $^-2 \leq d$ or d $^-2$

6 **a.** $x > 7$, when $x = 2.6$

     _____ > 7 _____

     b. $^-2 \leq d$, when $d = {}^-1$

     $^-2 \leq$ _____ _____

$x > {}^-1$

All numbers _____ than $^-1$ are solutions to the inequality $x > {}^-1$.

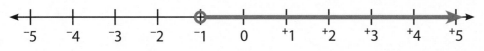

All numbers on the graph to the _____ of $^-1$ are solutions to the inequality $x > {}^-1$.

BUILD THE CONCEPT

TRY IT TOGETHER

Write each statement with the correct inequality symbol.

7 *b* is greater than or equal to 14.5

b ____ 14.5

8 ⁻3 is greater than *c*

⁻3 ____ *c*

9 The distance, *d*, is at most 10 miles.

10 The weight, *w*, is at least $18\frac{3}{4}$ pounds.

Determine if the given value is a solution for each inequality. Write *yes* or *no*.

11 $v \leq ^-9.6$, when $v = 8$

_____ $\leq ^-9.6$

_____

12 $204 < a$, when $a = 218$

$204 <$ _____

_____

WORK ON YOUR OWN

HOW TO

Write a Word Statement as an Inequality and Interpret an Inequality Symbol

Using Symbols	Using Words
• $1 < 4$	One is less than four.
• $1 \leq 4$	One is less than or equal to four.
• $4 > 1$	Four is greater than one.
• $4 \geq 1$	Four is greater than or equal to one.

SKILL BUILDING:
NEW AND REVIEW

Write each statement with the correct inequality symbol.

13 $10\frac{1}{3}$ is greater than n

14 p is less than or equal to 0

15 b is greater than or equal to $^-18$

16 $^-9.7$ is less than w

17 The speed allowed, s, is at most 60 miles per hour.

18 The temperature, t, is at least 65°F.

Determine if the given value is a solution for each inequality. Write *yes* or *no*.

19 $r \leq 9$, when $r = {}^-9$

20 $m \geq {}^-3.2$, when $m = {}^-4$

21 $5\frac{3}{4} \leq c$, when $c = 5\frac{3}{4}$

22 $15 > g$, when $g = {}^-9$

PROBLEM-SOLVING:
NEW AND REVIEW

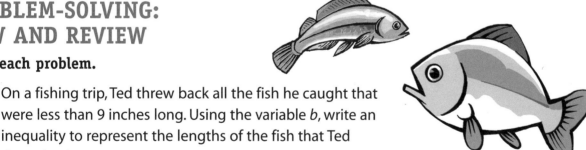

Solve each problem.

23 On a fishing trip, Ted threw back all the fish he caught that were less than 9 inches long. Using the variable b, write an inequality to represent the lengths of the fish that Ted threw back.

24 Using the information in problem 23 and the variable k, write an inequality to represent the lengths of the fish that Ted caught and kept.

25 On the fishing trip, Ted caught 4 more than twice the number of fish that Emma caught. Together, they caught 18 fish. Solve the equation, $2x + 4 = 18$, to find how many fish Emma caught. The variable, x, represents the number of fish Emma caught.

26 Stephen's report must be at least 8 pages. Using the variable r, write an inequality to represent the length required for Stephen's report. Is 8 a solution of the inequality? Explain.

Lesson 15

CHECK UP

Answer each question.

1 Which inequality represents the statement *n is less than 6*?

   a. $n < 6$ **b.** $6 - n$

   c. $n \leq 6$ **d.** $n > 6$

2 Which value is not a solution of $^-5 \leq v$?

   a. $^-1$ **b.** 0

   c. $^-6$ **d.** $^-5$

3 Which answer choice in problem 1 is the least reasonable? Explain.

_____

_____

The number of years, *y*, that Joshua has been snowboarding can be described by the inequality $y > 3$. Has Joshua been snowboarding for 3 years? for 3.5 years? Explain. _____

_____

_____

4 Write an inequality for each situation described below. Use *x* for the variable.

   a. The solutions to the inequality are only positive.

   _____

   b. The solutions to the inequality are only negative.

   _____

   c. The solutions to the inequality are both positive and negative.

   _____

End of Module Review

Name _____ Class _____ Date _____

Find the value of each exponential expression. [Lesson 1]

1 $^-(4)^2$

2 $(^-3)^3$

Evaluate each expression. [Lessons 2 and 3]

3 $12x$, when $x = 6$

4 $5 \cdot a$, when $a = ^-5$

5 $\dfrac{16(y - 2)}{(^-4)^2}$, when $y = 6$

Solve each equation. Then check the solution. [Lessons 4–6]

6 $46 = j + 50$

7 $h - 5.7 = 25.2$

8 $^-7m = 49$

9 $^-6 = \dfrac{q}{5}$

10 $\dfrac{s}{5} - 4 = 26$

11 $68 = 6t + 14$

Complete the input-output table. [Lesson 7]

12

In x	Function Rule y = 4x + 11	Out y
⁻1		
0		
1		
2		

Write each function rule. Then complete the input-output table. [Lesson 8]

13

x	y
⁻2	12
⁻1	6
1	⁻6
2	

$y = $ _____

14

x	y
⁻2	2
⁻1	3
1	5
2	

$y = $ _____

Solve the problem. [Lesson 9]

15) A bakery gives away 1 free pastry for every 3 purchased, 3 free pastries for every 9 purchased, and 5 free pastries for every 15 purchased. If Sarah receives 12 free pastries, how many did she purchase?

Use the coordinate plane for problems 16 and 17.
Write the ordered pair for each point. [Lesson 10]

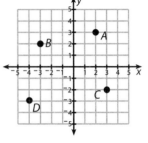

16) A

17) D

Complete the table. Then graph the linear equation. [Lesson 11]

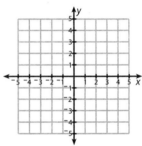

18)

x	y = ⁻2x + 1	y	(x, y)
⁻1			
0			
1			

Find the slope of the line and tell whether the slope is positive, negative, or zero. [Lesson 12]

19)

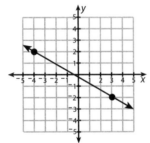

Write the prime factorization of each number using exponents. [Lesson 13]

20) 45

21) 900

Write each number in scientific notation. [Lesson 14]

22) 31,400

23) 2,530,000

Write each statement with the correct inequality symbol. [Lesson 15]

24) x is less than 6

25) Tom's mileage, m, is at least 32 miles per gallon.

Name _____ Class _____ Date _____

Lesson 1 Exponents

Write each product as an exponential expression.

1 ⁻5 × ⁻5 × ⁻5

2 2 × 2 × 2 × 2

3 ⁻3 × ⁻3 × ⁻3 × ⁻3 × ⁻3

4 7 × 7

5 ⁻4 × ⁻4 × ⁻4

6 ⁻1 × 8 × 8 × 8 × 8

7 ⁻10 × ⁻10 × ⁻10

8 ⁻1 × 6 × 6 × 6 × 6

9 ⁻4 × ⁻4 × ⁻4 × ⁻4 × ⁻4

Find the value of each exponential expression.

10 2^4

11 $⁻(9)^2$

12 3^6

13 $(⁻1)^3$

14 12^2

15 $(⁻2)^5$

Lesson 2 Variables and Expressions

Evaluate each expression.

1 $24x$, when $x = 3$

2 $\dfrac{⁻228}{t}$, when $t = 3$

3 $b + 86$, when $b = 31$

4 $s - 27$, when $s = 93$

5 $36 \cdot y$, when $y = ⁻6$

6 $a + 12$, when $a = ⁻7$

7 $a + 6$, when $a = 65$

8 $25 \cdot x$, when $x = ⁻5$

9 $k + 34$, when $k = 12$

10 $\dfrac{t}{2}$, when $t = 36$

11 $b - 35$, when $b = 14$

12 $16 - z$, when $z = 12$

13 $\dfrac{t}{3}$, when $t = 21$

14 $\dfrac{v}{5}$, when $v = 75$

15 $\dfrac{240}{u}$, when $u = ⁻30$

Name _____ Class _____ Date _____

Lesson 3 Evaluating Expressions Using Order of Operations
Evaluate each expression.

1 $14 - (^-5 + x)^2$, when $x = 3$

2 $\dfrac{9(8 + b)}{3}$, when $b = ^-3$

3 $\dfrac{^-228}{t} + (^-5)^2$, when $t = 4$

4 $3(6 - a^3)$, when $a = 3$

5 $4(m - 3.2)$, when $m = 9.7$

6 $\dfrac{5(h + 3^2)}{^-3}$, when $h = 3$

7 $8 + \dfrac{t}{5} \times 10$, when $t = 20$

8 $28 + 3a - 2$, when $a = 11$

9 $55 - 8 \times 2 + \dfrac{38}{m}$, when $m = 2$

10 $\dfrac{4x}{2} + 9$, when $x = 5$

Lesson 4 Solving One-Step Equations Using Addition and Subtraction
Solve each equation. Then check the solution.

1 $x + ^-6 = 4$

2 $y - 9 = ^-6$

3 $m + ^-3 = ^-8$

4 $p - 5 = 4$

5 $12 = n + ^-5$

6 $4 = x + 10$

7 $b + ^-62 = ^-31$

8 $15.4 = m - 3.4$

9 $q - 34 = 5$

10 $x + 7.8 = 10$

11 $a + ^-6 = 11$

12 $d - 19.2 = 5.8$

13 $n - 29 = 74$

14 $60 = t + 35$

15 $c - 5.3 = 2.4$

Name _____ Class _____ Date _____

Lesson 5 Solving One-Step Equations Using Multiplication and Division
Solve each equation. Then check the solution.

1 $^-6x = 18$

2 $\dfrac{y}{3} = 12$

3 $^-4m = 24$

4 $^-5t = 100$

5 $\dfrac{x}{8.2} = 6$

6 $^-8y = ^-72$

7 $^-4a = ^-48$

8 $\dfrac{b}{30} = 4$

9 $^-8 = \dfrac{t}{4}$

10 $70 = 5z$

11 $^-17n = ^-102$

12 $2w = 58$

13 $\dfrac{s}{100} = \dfrac{3}{5}$

14 $^-162 = ^-9p$

15 $3m = 63$

Lesson 6 Solving Two-Step Equations
Solve each equation. Then check the solution.

1 $5x + 4 = ^-6$

2 $\dfrac{y}{3} + 6 = 9$

3 $21 = 2m + 7$

4 $6p - 5 = 13$

5 $\dfrac{n}{7} + 5 = ^-2$

6 $^-5w - 1 = 24$

7 $^-3x + 5 = 11$

8 $15 = 2a + 7$

9 $2j + 7 = ^-5$

10 $\dfrac{g}{2} + 1 = 3$

11 $\dfrac{v}{5} + 2 = ^-6$

12 $1 = \dfrac{h}{4} - 5$

13 $4 = \dfrac{m}{5} + 13$

14 $6d - 3 = 27$

15 $3 + \dfrac{k}{2} = 2$

Name _____ Class _____ Date _____

Lesson 7 Input-Output Tables

Complete each input-output table.

1

In x	Function Rule y = 2x − 2	Out y
⁻1		
0		
1		
2		

2

In x	Function Rule y = ⁻2x + 10	Out y
⁻1		
0		
1		
2		

3

In x	Function Rule y = ⁻3x	Out y
⁻1		
0		
1		
2		

4

In x	Function Rule y = 3x + 2	Out y
⁻1		
0		
1		
2		

Lesson 8 Function Rules

Write each function rule. Then complete the input-output table.

1

x	y
⁻2	1
⁻1	2
1	4
2	

y =

2

x	y
⁻2	10
⁻1	5
1	⁻5
2	

y =

3

x	y
⁻2	⁻4
⁻1	⁻3
1	⁻1
2	

y =

4

x	y
⁻2	⁻3
⁻1	⁻2
1	0
2	

y =

5

x	y
⁻2	⁻4
⁻1	⁻2
1	2
2	

y =

6

x	y
⁻2	⁻8
⁻1	⁻4
1	4
2	

y =

7

x	y
⁻6	⁻2
⁻3	⁻1
0	0
3	

y =

8

x	y
⁻2	6
⁻1	3
0	0
1	

y =

9

x	y
0	10
10	20
20	30
30	

y =

Name _____ Class _____ Date _____

Lesson 9 Problem-Solving: Using a Table

Solve each problem.

1 There are 12 tennis balls in 4 containers, 18 tennis balls in 6 containers, and 24 tennis balls in 8 containers. How many can fit into 15 containers?

2 Bernardo opens a savings account with $50, and Sarah opens an account with $75. They each deposit money into their accounts. When Bernardo has $75 in his account, Sarah has $100 in hers. When Bernardo has $100 in his savings account, Sarah has $125. How much money will be in Sarah's savings account when Bernardo's savings account has $200?

3 Mr. Martinez is buying pizza for a fund-raiser. Two pizzas cost $16, 6 pizzas cost $48, and 10 pizzas cost $80. How many pizzas can Mr. Martinez buy with $136?

Lesson 10 Coordinate Plane

Use the coordinate plane for problems 1–16. Write the ordered pair for each point.

1 A

2 B

3 C

4 D

5 E

6 F

7 G

8 H

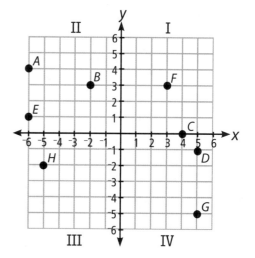

Graph each point on the coordinate plane.

9 $I(3, {}^-1)$

10 $J(2, 5)$

11 $K(0, 5)$

12 $L({}^-1, {}^-4)$

13 $M(1, 1)$

14 $N(2, {}^-5)$

15 $O({}^-5, {}^-5)$

16 $P({}^-4, 5)$

Name _____ Class _____ Date _____

Lesson 11 Graphing Linear Equations

Complete each table. Then graph the linear equation.

1 $y = x + 4$

In x	Function Rule y = x + 4	Out y	(x, y)
⁻2			
⁻1			
0			

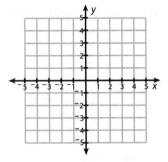

2 $y = 3x - 1$

In x	Function Rule y = 3x − 1	Out y	(x, y)
⁻1			
0			
1			

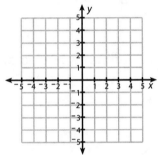

Lesson 12 Finding Slope

Find the slope of each line and tell whether the slope is positive, negative, or zero.

1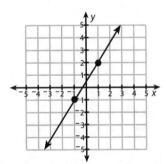

2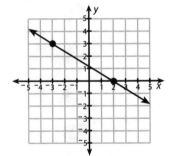

Graph the linear equation and find the slope of the line.

3 $y = 2x + 4$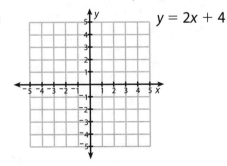

4 $y = x + 4$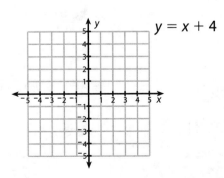

Name _____ Class _____ Date _____

Lesson 13 Prime Factorization

Write the prime factorization of each number using exponents.

1 20

2 56

3 21

4 70

5 50

6 35

7 28

8 36

9 60

10 72

11 33

12 100

13 75

14 18

15 340

Lesson 14 Powers of Ten and Scientific Notation

Write each number in scientific notation.

1 45,600

2 35,700,000

3 130

4 392,000,000

5 47,000,000

6 575,000

Write each number in standard form.

7 7.19×10^6

8 6.03×10^3

9 1.25×10^5

10 9.1×10^4

11 4.5×10^9

12 5×10^{12}

Name _____ Class _____ Date _____

Lesson 15 Inequalities

Write each statement with the correct inequality symbol.

1 14 is less than or equal to x

2 p is greater than $2\frac{1}{2}$

3 7 is greater than or equal to t

4 $^-9$ is less than y

5 t is at least 80°F

6 q is at most $^-99$

7 u is at most 10

8 t is at least 1

Determine if the given value is a solution for each inequality. Write _yes_ or _no_.

9 $y < 8$, when $y = {}^-10$

10 $t \leq {}^-9$, when $t = {}^-9$

11 $^-25 < b$, when $b = {}^-30$

12 $\frac{3}{4} \geq h$, when $h = \frac{1}{4}$

13 $\frac{1}{2} \leq p$, when $p = \frac{2}{5}$

14 $w > 3$, when $w = 4$

Glossary

algebraic expression

an expression containing one or more numerals, one or more variables, and one or more operations

base

the number used as a factor in repeated multiplication

composite number

a whole number that has more than two factors

coordinate plane

a plane formed by two number lines intersecting at right angles

equation

a mathematical sentence formed by placing an equal sign between two expressions

exponent

a number that indicates how many times a base is used as a factor in repeated multiplication

function

a pairing of input and output values in which each input value is paired with exactly one output value

function rule

an equation that shows how an input value, x, and an output value, y, are related

inequality

a mathematical sentence that contains one of the symbols >, < , ≥, or ≤

input-output table

a table that shows how an input value, x, is paired with an output value, y

linear equation

an equation whose graph is a straight line

ordered pair

a pair of numbers used to locate a point on a coordinate plane

origin

the point where the x-axis and y-axis intersect

prime factorization

a factorization of a whole number using only its prime factors

prime number

a whole number that has exactly two factors, 1 and the number itself

quadrants

the four sections formed by the intersection of the x-axis and y-axis

rise

the vertical change between any two points on a line

run

the horizontal change between any two points on a line

scientific notation

a number expressed as the product of two factors; the first factor is a number greater than or equal to 1 and less than 10, and the second is a power of 10

sequence

a list of numbers that follows a mathematical rule or equation

slope

the ratio of the vertical change to the horizontal change between any two points on a line

solution

a number that when substituted for a variable in an equation, results in a true statement

Glossary

term
one number or value in a sequence

variable
a letter or symbol that represents a number

x-**axis**
the horizontal number line of a coordinate plane

y-**axis**
the vertical number line of a coordinate plane

Name _____ Class _____ Date _____

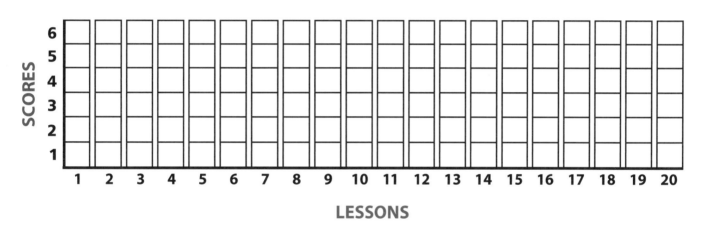

WORK ON YOUR OWN

PROGRESS CHART

Chart with SCORES (1–6) on vertical axis and LESSONS (1–20) on horizontal axis.

LESSONS